VOX

First
French Picture
Dictionary

500 Brightly Illustrated Words to Start Speaking French

McGraw·Hill

New York   Chicago   San Francisco   Lisbon   London   Madrid   Mexico City
Milan   New Delhi   San Juan   Seoul   Singapore   Sydney   Toronto

Table of contents
Table des matières

The McGraw·Hill Companies

1 2 3 4 5 6 7 8 9 0   MPC/MPC   3 2 1 0 9 8 7 6 5 4

ISBN 0-07-143305-8

Illustrations by Sívia Pla Payà

McGraw-Hill books are available at special quantity discounts to use as premiums and sales promotions, or for use in corporate training programs. For more information, please write to the Director of Special Sales, Professional Publishing, McGraw-Hill, Two Penn Plaza, New York, NY 10121-2298. Or contact your local bookstore.

Good morning!
Bonjour!

toys
les jouets

alarm clock
le réveil

curtain
le rideau

pajamas
le pyjama

pillow
l'oreiller

bed
le lit

blanket
la couverture

rug
le tapis

slippers
les pantoufles

socks
les chaussettes

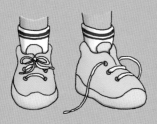

sneakers
les baskets

to sleep
dormir

to get dressed
s'habiller

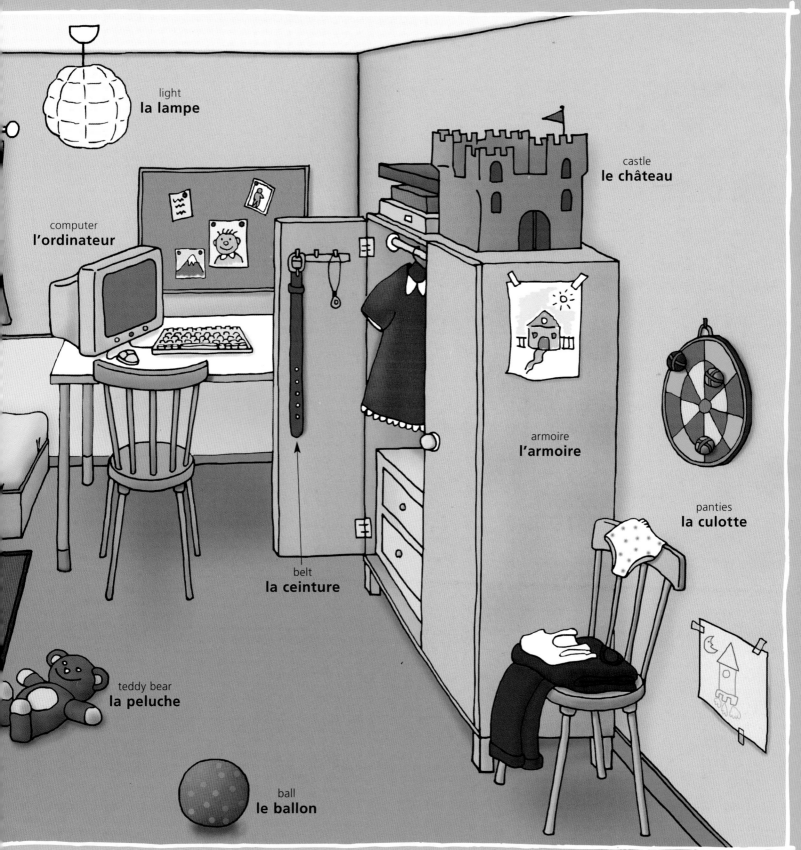

light
la lampe

computer
l'ordinateur

castle
le château

armoire
l'armoire

belt
la ceinture

panties
la culotte

teddy bear
la peluche

ball
le ballon

In the bathroom
Dans la salle de bains

soap
le savon

arm
le bras

shower
la douche

sponge
l'éponge

bathtub
la baignoire

toothbrush
la brosse à dents

to comb
peigner

hair dryer
le séchoir

hairbrush
la brosse à cheveux

mirror
le miroir

head
la téte

toothpaste
le dentifrice

comb
le peigne

toilet
le W.-C.

sink
le lavabo

hand
la main

knee
le genou

toilet paper
le papier hygiénique

towel
la serviette de bain

leg
la jambe

foot
le pied

Breakfast time!
Le petit déjeuner

radio
le poste de radio

fork
la fourchette

cereal
les céréales

toast
le toast

spoon
la cuillère

cup
la tasse

milk
le lait

knife
le couteau

newspaper
le journal

to hug
prendre dans ses bras

orange juice
le jus d'orange

to eat
manger

tray
le plateau

sugar
le sucre

yogurt
le yaourt

cookies
les biscuits

jam
la marmelade

butter
le beurre

door
la porte

cat
le chat

9

In the street
Dans la rue

MARCHAND DE FLEURS

sign
le panneau

streetlight
le réverbère

newsstand
le kiosque à journaux

magazine
la revue

bus
l'autobus

blind man
l'aveugle

bus stop
l'arrêt de bus

cell phone
le téléphone portable

to read
lire

to talk
parler

BOULANGERIE

truck
camion

car
la voiture

traffic light
le feu

garbage can
la poubelle

scooter
la mobylette

police officer
l'agent de police

mailbox
la boîte aux lettres

letter
la lettre

mail carrier
le facteur

In the classroom
Dans la salle de classe

blackboard
le tableau

calendar
le calendrier

map
la carte

chair
la chaise

desk
le bureau

eraser
l'effaceur

chalk
la craie

ruler
la règle

pencil
le crayon

pen
le stylo

folder
la chemise

sheet
la feuille

to study
étudier

scissors
les ciseaux

to write
écrire

teacher
l'instituteur

books
les livres

drawing
le dessin

pencil case
la trousse

coat hook
la patère

notebook
le cahier

backpack
le sac à dos

eraser
la gomme

wastepaper basket
la corbeille à papier

The music class
En cours de musique

score
la partition

flute
la flûte traversiére

maracas
les maracas

chorus
le chœur

guitar
la guitare

xylophone
le xylophone

tambourine
le tambourin

drum
le tambour

piano
le piano

to sing
chanter

to hear
entendre

notes
les notes

stereo
la chaîne hi-fi

trumpet
la trompette

cymbals
les cymbales

triangle
le triangle

violin
le violon

cello
le violoncelle

conductor
le chef d'orchestre

In the park
Au jardin public

jungle gym
la cage à poules

grass
l'herbe

swing
la balançoire

slide
le toboggan

roller skates
les patins

boy
le petit garçon

fountain
la fontaine

bicycle
la bicyclette

friends
les amis

to drink
boire

to run
courir

bench
le banc

pigeon
le pigeon

girl
la petite fille

bucket
le seau

see-saw
la bascule

skateboard
la planche à roulettes

jump rope
la corde

sandwich
le sandwich

swan
le cygne

pond
la mare

Happy birthday!
Bon anniversaire!

drink
le rafraîchissement

mask
le masque

cand
la bou

cake
le gateau

chocolate
le chocolate

tablecloth
la nappe

doll
la poupé

present
le cadeau

candy
les bonbons

to kiss
embrasser

to blow
souffler

camera
l'appareil photo

balloon
le ballon

chips
les chips

glass
le verre

sandwich
le sandwich

plate
l'assiette

napkin
la serviette

scooter
la patinette

Shopping
Les courses

BOUCHERIE

MARCHAND DE FRUITS

meat
la viande

sausages
les saucisses

cheese
le fromage

ham
le jambon

fruit
le fruit

vegetables
les légumes

basket
le panier

MARCHAND DE FLEURS

plant
la plante

flower
la fleur

money
l'argent

shopping list
la liste des courses

to buy
acheter

VOLAILLER

eggs
les œufs

chicken
le poulet

cart
le chariot

mussels
les moules

octopus
la poulpe

fish
le poisson

Clothes
Les vêtements

dress
la robe

bag
le sac

skirt
la jupe

shirt
la chemise

sweater
le pull-over

jacket
le blouson

t-shirt
le tee-shirt

sales clerk
la vendeuse

label
l'étiquette

shoe
la chaussure

big
grand

small
petit

clothes
les vêtements

fitting room
le salon d'essayage

mirror
le miroir

underpants
le caleçon

hanger
le portemanteau

coat
le manteau

handbag
le sac à main

pants
le pantalon

At the grocery store
Au supermarché

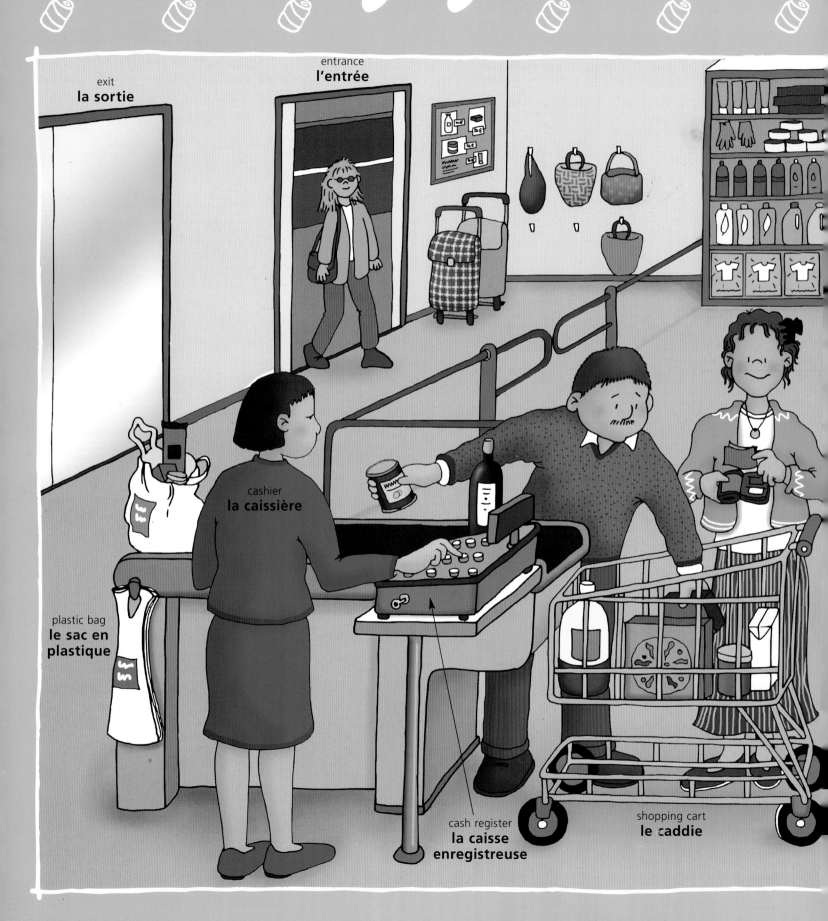

exit
la sortie

entrance
l'entrée

cashier
la caissière

plastic bag
le sac en plastique

cash register
la caisse enregistreuse

shopping cart
le caddie

price
le prix

credit card
la carte de crédit

to take
prendre

jar
le bocal

can
la boîte de conserve

frozen food
les surgelés

bottle
la bouteille

melon
le melon

pineapple
l'ananas

scale
la balance

banana
la banane

potato
la pomme de terre

carrot
la carotte

detergent
le détersif

In the kitchen
Dans la cuisine

clock
la pendule

range hood
l'extracteur

sponge
l'éponge

pot
la casserole

frying pan
la poêle

cupboard
**la placard
de cuisine**

oil
l'huile

outlet
**la prise
de courant**

stove
la cuisinière

microwave
le four micro-ondes

washing machine
**la machine
à laver**

to wash up
laver

food
les aliments

to cook
cuisiner

sink
l'évier

plate
l'assiette

refrigerator
le frigo

telephone
le téléphone

table
la table

broom
le balai

garbage can
la poubelle

cloth
le chiffon

Le monde du travail
Jobs

dentist
la dentiste

hairdresser
le coiffeur

dancer
la danseuse

doctor
le médecin

nurse
l'infirmière

GARAGE

cook
le cuisinier

mechanic
le mécanicien

waiter
le serveur

to cure
guérir
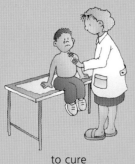

to paint
peindre

to sweep
balayer

fireman
le pompier

student
l'étudiante

carpenter
le menuisier

construction worker
l'ouvrier

gardener
le jardinier

painter
le peintre

At the zoo
Au jardin zoologique

vet
la vétérinaire

cub
le lionceau

elephant
l'éléphant

trunk
la trompe

monkey
le singe

turtle
la tortue

tail
la queue

ice cream
la glace

wheelchair
le fauteuil roulant

butterfly
le papillon

parrot
le perroquet

giraffe
la girafe

dolphin
le dauphin

tiger
le tigre

lion
le lion

seal
le phoque

penguin
le manchot

bear
l'ours

15

Les fêtes de mardi gras

singer
la chanteuse

wizard
l'enchanteur

witch
la sorcière

pirate
le pirate

ghost
le fantôme

robot
le robot

king
le roi

queen
la reine

cowboy
le cow-boy

costumes
les déguisements

to dance
danser

to laugh
rire

camcorder
le caméscope

clown
le clown

fairy
la fée

devil
le diable

Transportation 16
Les modes de transport

plane
l'avion

lighthouse
le phare

bus
l'autobus

car
la voiture

road
la chaussée

tunnel
le tunnel

train
le train

track
la voie

to drive
conduire

to fly
voler

to sail
naviguer

light aircraft
le petit avion

sailboat
le voilier

ship
le navire

helicopter
l'hélicoptère

island
l'île

boat
la barque

hot-air balloon
le ballon

waterskiing
le ski nautique

speedboat
la vedette

In the garden
Au jardin

orange
l'orange

pear
la poire

lemon
le citron

scarecrow
l'épouvantail

watermelon
la pastèque

cauliflower
la choufleur

lettuce
la laitue

pumpkin
la citrouille

to water
arroser

ladybug
la coccinelle

peas
les petits pois

apple
la pomme

bird
l'oiseau

shovel
le pelle

faucet
le robinet

horse
le cheval

bread
le pain

axe
la hache

watering can
l'arrosoir

hose
le tuyau d'arrosage

tomato
la tomate

firewood
le bois à brûler

sack
le sac

18

En campagne

house
la maison

chaperone
le chaperon

boot
la botte

cap
la casquette

snail
l'escargot

squirrel
l'écureil

to hike
faire une randonnée

nest
le nid

mountain
la montagne

forest
le bois

hill
la colline

fox
le renard

flower
la fleur

backpack
le sac à dos

stone
la pierre

water bottle
la gourde

pine cone
la pomme de pin

bee
l'abeille

ants
les fourmis

hroom
mpignon

At the beach
À la plage

kite
le cerf-volant

sky
le ciel

fish
le poisson

wave
la vague

beach umbrella
le parasol

sand castle
le château de sable

sand
le sable

sunglasses
les lunettes de soleil

towel
la serviette de bain

hot
chaud

to swim
nager

shell
la coquille

sun
le soleil

windsurfing
la planche à voile

lifeguard
le secouriste

sea
la mer

inner tube
la bouée

shovel
la pelle

bathing suit
le maillot de bain

bikini
le bikini

bucket
le seau

rake
le râteau

crab
le crabe

On the farm
À la ferme
20

straw
la paille

field
le champ

tractor
le tracteur

cow
la vache

mouse
la souris

farmer
le fermier

water
l'eau

duck
le canard

rabbit
le lapin

peacock
le paon

dog
le chien

sheep
le mouton

honey
le miel

to plant
planter

cat
le chat

door
la porte

window
la fenêtre

pig
le cochon

rooster
le coq

hen
la poule

chicks
les poussins

21

At night
La nuit

moon
la lune

star
l'etoile

chimney
la cheminée

bat
la chauve-souris

roof
le toit

owl
le hibou

cabin
la cabane

steps
les marches

firewood
le bois à brûler

branch
la branche

campfire
le feu de camp

to yawn
bâiller

darkness
l'obscurité

to dream
rêver

tree
l'arbre

light
la lumière

flashlight
**la lampe
de poche**

rock
le rocher

frog
la grenouille

river
le fleuve

22 Christmas
Le Noël

nativity
**la crèche
de Noël**

son
le fils

stocking
le bas

card
la carte

candy
les bonbons

grandmother
la grand-mère

father
le père

mother
la mère

angel
l'ange

fire
le feu

brother
le frère

sister
la sœur

decorations
les décorations

Santa Claus
le père Noël

fireplace
le foyer

star
l'étoile

grandfather
le grand-père

tinsel
les guirlandes de Noël

daughter
la fille

Christmas tree
le sapin de Noël

In the snow
Les sports d'hiver

cloud
le nuage

glove
le gant

winter hat
le bonnet de neige

jacket
l'anorak

ice
la glace

skis
les skis

snowball
la boule de neige

scarf
l'écharpe

coat
le manteau

to ski
faire du ski

to snow
neiger

cold
froid

chair lift
le remote-pente

skier
le skieur

pine tree
le sapin

snowman
le bonhomme de neige

snow
la neige

sweater
le pull-over

sled
la luge

My face
Mon visage

pigtails
les couettes

forehead
le front

ear
l'oreille

mouth
la bouche

shoulder
l'épaule

chin
le menton

fingernail
l'ongle

arm
le bras

happy
content

sad
triste

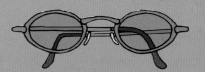

glasses
les lunettes

eyebrow
le sourcil

hair
les cheveux

eye
l'œil

nose
le nez

cheek
la joue

neck
le cou

thumb
le pouce

finger
le doigt

hand
la main

elbow
le coude

25 Parts of the day Jour et nuit

morning **le matin**	afternoon **l'après-midi**	night **la nuit**

26 Weather Le temps

sun
le soleil   wind
le vent   rainbow
l'arc-en-ciel   rain
la pluie   snow
la neige

27 Days of the week La semaine

Tuesday
mardi   Thursday
jeudi   Saturday
samedi

Monday
lundi   Wednesday
mercredi   Friday
vendredi   Sunday
dimanche

28 Seasons Les saisons de l'année

spring
le printemps   summer
l'été   autumn
l'automne   winter
l'hiver

29 Numbers **Les numéros**

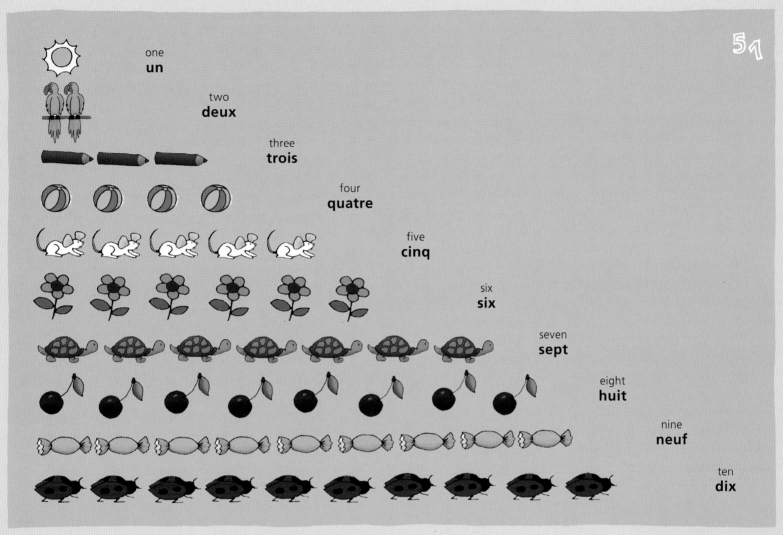

one
un

two
deux

three
trois

four
quatre

five
cinq

six
six

seven
sept

eight
huit

nine
neuf

ten
dix

30 Colors **Les couleurs**

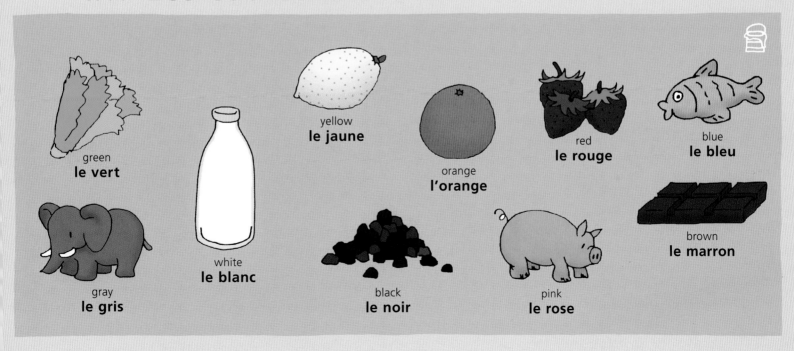

green
le vert

white
le blanc

yellow
le jaune

orange
l'orange

red
le rouge

blue
le bleu

gray
le gris

black
le noir

pink
le rose

brown
le marron

Indexes
Indices

French-English Glossary and Pronunciation

Look at the pronunciation guide in parentheses after each French word or expression in this word list. It will teach you to pronounce the French words and phrases as the French do. When you pronounce the guides out loud, read them as you would read words and syllables in English.

Notice that French has some sounds that are not found in English. Here are the symbols we use to show these sounds. Some of them are shown as capital letters, which will help you spot them easily.

R The French **r** (as in **bonjour**, **Ro**be**rt**) is pronounced at the back of the throat, a bit like gargling.

uh The letter combinations **eu**, **œu** (as in **peu**, **œufs**), and sometimes the letters **e** (as in **de**, **je**, **que**) and **o** (as in **port**, **accord**, **sorbet**), are spelled **uh** in the guides. To say this sound, hold your tongue as if to make the *ay* sound and round your lips as if to make the *o* sound.

ERR This sound is a more "open" version of the one above (**uh**). It is usually found in the letter combinations -**eur** or -**œur** (as in **chanteur**, **leur**, **sœur**).

U To pronounce the French **u** (usually a single **u** in spelling, as in **tu**, **rue**, **jupe**), hold your tongue as if to make the *ee* sound and round your lips as if to make the *o* sound.

A^n, I^n, O^n French also has several sounds called *nasalized* vowels, spelled with the letters **a**, **e**, **i**, **o** immediately before the letter **n** (as in **manteau**, **main**, **mon**). Pronounce these vowels through your mouth and nose at the same time. They are shown in the guides with the symbols at the left.

Hints: When you read the pronunciation guides aloud, always pronounce a single *e* like the *e* in the English word *let*. The letter (sound) **a** has been written **ah**; in French, the letter **a** always sounds like the *a* in *father*. All French words give a slight emphasis to their final syllable. Please note that the number following the English translation refers to the unit, not the page.

A

l'abeille (f.) (lah-bay) bee 18

acheter (ahsh-tay) to buy 9

l'agent de police (m.) (lah-jA^n-duh-po-lees) police officer 4

les aliments (m.) (lay-zah-lee-mA^n) food 12

les amis (m.) (lay-zah-mee) friends 7

l'ananas (m.) (lah-nah-nahs) pineapple 11

l'ange (m.) (lA^{n}j) angel 22

l'anorak (m.) (lah-nuh-Rahk) jacket 23

l'appareil photo (m.) (lah-pah-Ray-fuh-to) camera 8

l'après-midi (m.) (lah-pRay-mee-dee) afternoon 25

l'arbre (m.) (lahRbR) tree 21

l'arc-en-ciel (m.) (lahRk-A^n-syel) rainbow 26

l'argent (m.) (lahR-jA^n) money 9

l'armoire (f.) (lahR-mwahR) armoire 1

l'arrêt de bus (m.) (lah-Ray-duh-bUs) bus stop 4

arroser (ah-Ro-zay) to water 17

l'arrosoir (m.) (lah-Ro-zwahR) watering can 17

l'assiette (f.) (lah-syet) plate 8, 12

l'autobus (m.) (luh-tuh-bUs) bus 4, 16

l'automne (m.) (luh-tuhn) autumn 28

l'aveugle (m.) (lah-vuhgl) blind man 4

l'avion (m.) (lah-vyO^n) plane 16

B

la baignoire (lah-be-nywahR) bathtub 2

bâiller (bai-yay) to yawn 21

le balai (luh-bah-lay) broom 12

la balance (lah-bah-lA^{n}s) scale 11

la balançoire (lah-bah-lA^n-swahR) swing 7

balayer (bah-lay-yay) to sweep 13

le ballon (luh-bah-lO^n) ball 1; balloon 8; hot-air balloon 16

la banane (lah-bah-nahn) banana 11

le banc (luh-bA^n) bench 7

la barque (lah-bahRk) boat 16

le bas (luh-bah) stocking 22

la bascule (lah-bas-kUl) seesaw 7

les baskets (m.) (lay-bahs-ket) sneakers 1

le beurre (luh-bERR) butter 3

la bicyclette (lah-bee-see-klet) bicycle 7

le bikini (luh-bee-kee-nee) bikini 19

les biscuits (m.) (lay-bee-skwee) cookies 3

le blanc (luh-blA^n) white 30

le bleu (luh-bluh) blue 30

le blouson (luh-bloo-zO^n) jacket 10

le bocal (luh-bo-kahl) jar 11

boire (bwahR) to drink 7

le bois (luh-bwah) forest 18

le bois à brûler (luh-bwah-ah-bRU-lay) firewood 17, 21

la boîte aux lettres (lah-bwah-to-letR) mailbox 4

la boîte de conserve (lah-bwaht-duh-kO^n-seRv) can 11

Bon anniversaire! (buh-nah-nee-veR-seR) Happy Birthday! 8

les bonbons (m.) (lay-bO^n-bO^n) candy 8, 22

le bonhomme de neige (luh-buh-nuhm-duh-nej) snowman 23

Bonjour! (bO^n-jooR) Good Morning! 1

le bonnet de neige (luh-buh-nay-duh-nej) winter hat 23

la botte (lah-buht) boot 18

la bouche (lah-boosh) mouth 24

la boucherie (lah-boo-shRee) butcher's 9

la bouée (lah-boo-ay) inner tube 19

la bougie (lah-boo-jee) candle 8

la boulangerie (lah-boo-lA^n-jRee) bakery 4

la boule de neige (lah-bool-duh-nej) snowball 23

la bouteille (lah-boo-tay) bottle 11

la branche (lah-bRA^{n}sh) branch 21

le bras (luh-bRah) arm 2, 24

la brosse à cheveux (lah-bRuh-sah-shuh-vuh) hairbrush 2

la brosse à dents (lah-bRuh-sah-dA^n) toothbrush 2

le **bureau** (luh-bU-Ro) desk 5

C

la **cabane** (lah-kah-bahn) cabin 21

le **caddie** (luh-kah-dee) shopping cart 11

le **cadeau** (luh-kah-do) present 8

la **cage à poules** (lah-kahj-ah-pool] jungle gym 7

le **cahier** (luh-kah-yay) notebook 5

la **caisse enregistreuse** (lah-kes-A^n-Re-jees-tRuhz) cash register 11

la **caissière** (lah-keh-syeR) cashier 11

le **caleçon** (luh-kahl-sO^n) underpants 10

le **calendrier** (luh-kahl-A^n-dRee-ay) calendar 5

le **caméscope** (luh-kah-may-skuhp) camcorder 15

la **campagne** (lah-kA^n-pahny) country 18

le **camion** (luh-kah-myO^n) truck 4

le **canard** (luh-kah-nahR) duck 20

la **carotte** (lah-kah-Ruht) carrot 11

la **carte** (lah-kahRt) map 5, card 22

la **carte de crédit** (lah-kahRt-duh-kRe-dee) credit card 11

la **casquette** (lah-kah-sket) cap 18

la **casserole** (lah-kahs-Rol) pot 12

la **ceinture** (lah-sI^n-tUR) belt 1

les **céréales (f.)** (lay-say-Ray-ahl) cereal 3

le **cerf-volant** (luh-seR-vuh-lA^n) kite 19

la **chaîne hi-fi** (lah-shen-ee-fee) stereo 6

la **chaise** (lah-shez) chair 5

le **champ** (luh-shA^n) field 20

le **champignon** (luh-shA^n-pee-nyO^n) mushroom 18

chanter (shA^n-tay) to sing 6

la **chanteuse** (lah-shA^n-tuhz) singer 15

le **chaperon** (luh-sha-peR-O^n) chaperone 18

le **chariot** (luh-sha-Ryo) cart 9

le **chat** (luh-shah) cat 3, 20

le **château** (luh-shah-toh) castle 1

le **château de sable** (luh-shah-tod-sahbl) sand castle 19

chaud (sho) hot 19

la **chaussée** (lah-sho-say) road 16

les **chaussettes (f.)** (lay-sho-set) socks 1

la **chaussure** (lah-sho-sUR) shoe 10

la **chauve-souris** (lah-shov-soo-Ree) bat 21

le **chef d'orchestre** (luh-shef-duhR-kestR) conductor 6

la **cheminée** (lah-shuh-mee-nay) chimney 21

la **chemise** (lah-shuh-meez) folder 5; shirt 10

le **cheval** (luh-shuh-vahl) horse 17

les **cheveux (m.)** (lay-shuh-vuh) hair 24

le **chien** (luh-shyI^n) dog 20

le **chiffon** (luh-shee-fO^n) cloth 12

le **chiot** (luh-shyo) puppy 14

les **chips (m.)** (lay-sheeps) chips 8

le **chocolat** (luh-sho-ko-lah) chocolate 8

le **chœur** (luh-kERR) chorus 6

la **choufleur** (lah-shoo-flERR) cauliflower 17

le **ciel** (luh-syel) sky 19

cinq (sI^{n}k) five 29

les **ciseaux (m.)** (lay-see-zo) scissors 5

le **citron** (luh-see-tRO^n) lemon 17

la **citrouille** (lah-see-tRoo-ee) pumpkin 17

le **clown** (luh-kloon) clown 15

la **coccinelle** (lah-kuhk-see-nel) ladybug 17

le **cochon** (luh-kuh-shO^n) pig 20

le **coiffeur** (luh-kwah-fERR) hairdresser 13

la **colline** (lah-kuhl-een) hill 18

conduire (kO^n-dweeR) to drive 16

content (kO^n-tA^n) happy 24

le **coq** (luh-kuhk) rooster 20

la **coquille** (lah-kuh-kee) shell 19

la **corbeille à papier** (lah-kuhR-bay-ah-pah-pyay) wastepaper basket 5

la **corde** (lah-kuhRd) jump rope 7

le **cou** (luh-koo) neck 24

le **coude** (luh-kood) elbow 24

les **couettes (f.)** (lay-kwet) pigtails 24

les **couleurs (f.)** (lay-koo-lERR) colors 30

courir (koo-ReeR) to run 7

le **cours de musique** (luh-kooR-duh-mU-zeek) music class 6

les **courses (f.)** (lay-kooRs) shopping 9

le **couteau** (luh-koo-to) knife 3

la **couverture** (lah-koo-veR-tUR) blanket 1

le **cow-boy** (luh-ko-buhy) cowboy 15

le **crabe** (luh-kRahb) crab 19

la **craie** (lah-kRay) chalk 5

le **crayon** (luh-kRay-O^n) pencil 5

la **crèche de Noël** (lah-kResh-duh-no-el) nativity 22

la **cuillère** (lah-kwee-yeR) spoon 3

la **cuisine** (lah-kwee-zeen) kitchen 12

cuisiner (kwee-zee-nay) to cook 12

le **cuisinier** (luh-kwee-zee-nye) cook 13

la **cuisinière** (lah-kwee-zee-nyeR) stove 12

la **culotte** (lah-kU-luht) panties 1

le **cygne** (luh-see-nyuh) swan 7

les **cymbales (f.)** (lay-sI^n-bahl) cymbals 6

D

danser (dA^n-say) to dance 15

la **danseuse** (lah-dA^n-suhz) dancer 13

le **dauphin** (luh-doh-fI^n) dolphin 14

les **décorations (f.)** (lay-day-ko-Rah-syO^n) decorations 22

les **déguisements (m.)** (lay-day-geez-mA^n) costumes 15

le **dentifrice** (luh-dA^n-tee-fRees) toothpaste 2

la **dentiste** (lah-dA^n-teest) dentist 13

le **dessin** (luh-des-sI^n) drawing 5

le **détersif** (luh-day-teR-seef) detergent 11

deux (duh) two 29

le **diable** (luh-dyahbl) devil 15

le **dimanche** (luh-dee-mA^{n}sh) Sunday 27

dix (dees) ten 29

le **doigt** (luh-dwah) finger 24

dormir (duhR-meeR) to sleep 1

la **douche** (lah-doosh) shower 2

E

l'**eau (f.)** (lo) water 20

l'**écharpe (f.)** (lay-shahRp) scarf 23

écrire (ay-kReeR) to write 5

l'**écureil (m.)** (lay-kU-Ruhy) squirrel 18

l'**effaceur (m.)** (lay-fah-sERR) eraser 5

l'**éléphant (m.)** (lay-lay-fA^n) elephant 14

embrasser (A^n-bRah-say) to kiss 8

l'**enchanteur (m.)** (lA^n-shA^n-tERR) wizard 15

entendre (A^n-tA^{n}dR) to hear 6

l'**entrée (f.)** (lA^n-tRay) entrance 11

l'**épaule (f.)** (lay-pol) shoulder 24

l'**éponge (f.)** (lay-pO^{n}j) sponge 2, 12

l'**épouvantail (m.)** (lay-poo-vA^n-tai) scarecrow 17

l'escargot (m.) (les-kahR-go) snail 18

l'été (m.) (lay-tay) summer 28

l'étiquette (f.) (le-tee-ket) label 10

l'étoile (f.) (lay-twahl) star 21, 22

l'étudiante (f.) (lay-tU-dyAⁿt) student 13

étudier (ay-tU-dyay) to study 5

l'évier (m.) (lay-vyay) sink 12

l'extracteur (m.) (leks-tRahk-tERR) range hood 12

F

le facteur (luh-fahk-tERR) mail carrier 4

faire du ski (feR-dU-skee) to ski 23

faire une randonnée (feR-Un-RAⁿ-duh-nay) to hike 18

le fantôme (luh-fAⁿ-tom) ghost 15

le fauteuil roulant (luh-fo-tuhy-Roo-lAⁿ) wheelchair 14

la fée (lah-fay) fairy 15

la fenêtre (lah-fuh-netR) window 20

la ferme (lah-feRm) farm 20

le fermier (luh-feRm-yay) farmer 20

Les fêtes (f.) de Mardi Gras (lay-fet-duh-mahR-dee-grah) Carnival Time 15

le feu (luh-fuh) traffic light 4; fire 22

le feu de camp (luh-fuhd-kAⁿ) campfire 21

la feuille (lah-fuhy) sheet (of paper) 5

la fille (lah-feey) daughter 22

le fils (luh-fees) son 22

la fleur (lah-flERR) flower 9, 18

le fleuve (luh-fluhv) river 21

la flûte traversière (lah-flUt-tRah-veR-syeR) flute 6

la fontaine (lah-fOⁿ-ten) fountain 7

le four micro-ondes (luh-fooR-mee-kRo-Oⁿd) microwave 12

la fourchette (lah-fooR-shet) fork 3

les fourmis (f.) (lay-fooR-mee) ants 18

le foyer (luh-fwah-yay) fireplace 22

le frère (luh-fReR) brother 22

le frigo (luh-fRee-go) refrigerator 12

froid (fRwah) cold 23

le fromage (luh-fRo-maj) cheese 9

le front (luh-fROⁿ) forehead 24

le fruit (luh-fRwee) fruit 9

G

le gant (luh-gAⁿ) glove 23

le garage (luh-gah-Rahj) garage 13

le gateau (luh-gah-toh) cake 8

le genou (luh-jnoo) knee 2

la girafe (lah-jee-Rahf) giraffe 14

la glace (lah-glahs) ice cream 14; ice 23

la gomme (lah-guhm) eraser 5

la gourde (lah-gooRd) water bottle 18

grand (gRAⁿ) big 10

la grand-mère (lah-gRAⁿ-meR) grandmother 22

le grand-père (luh-gRAⁿ-peR) grandfather 22

la grenouille (lah-gRuh-nooy) frog 21

le gris (luh-gRee) gray 30

guérir (gay-ReeR) to cure 13

les guirlandes (f.) de Noël (lay-geeR-lahnd-duh-no-el) tinsel 22

la guitare (lah-gee-tahR) guitar 6

H

s'habiller (sah-bee-yay) to get dressed 1

la hache (lah-ahsh) axe 17

l'hélicoptère (m.) (lay-lee-kuhp-teR) helicopter 16

l'herbe (f.) (leRb) grass 7

le hibou (luh-ee-boo) owl 21

l'hiver (m.) (lee-veR) winter 23, 28

l'huile (f.) (lweel) oil 12

huit (weet) eight 29

I

l'île (f.) (leel) island 16

l'infirmière (f.) (IIⁿ-feeR-myeR) nurse 13

l'instituteur (m.) (IIⁿ-stee-tU-tERR) teacher 5

J

la jambe (lah-jAⁿb) leg 2

le jambon (luh-jAⁿ-bOⁿ) ham 9

le jardin (luh-jahR-dIⁿ) garden 17

le jardin public (luh-jahR-dIⁿ-pU-bleek) park 7

le jardin zoologique (luh-jahR-dIⁿ-zuh-uh-luh-jeek) zoo 14

le jardinier (luh-jahR-dee-nyay) gardener 13

le jaune (luh-jon) yellow 30

le jeudi (luh-juh-dee) Thursday 27

la joue (lah-joo) cheek 24

les jouets (m.) (lay-joo-ay) toys 1

le jour (luh-joor) day 25

le journal (luh-jooR-nahl) newspaper 3

la jupe (lah-jUp) skirt 10

le jus d'orange (m.) (luh-jU-duh-RAⁿj) orange juice 3

K

le kiosque à journaux (luh-kee-os-kah-joor-no) newsstand 4

L

le lait (luh-lay) milk 3

la laitue (lah-lay-tU) lettuce 17

la lampe (lah-lAⁿp) light 1

la lampe de poche (lah-lAⁿp-duh-puhsh) flashlight 21

le lapin (luh-lah-pIⁿ) rabbit 20

le lavabo (luh-lah-vah-bo) sink 2

laver (lah-vay) to wash 12

les légumes (m.) (lay-lay-gUm) vegetables 9

la lettre (lah-letR) letter 4

le lion (luh-lyOⁿ) lion 14

le lionceau (luh-lyOⁿ-so) cub 14

lire (leeR) to read 4

la liste des courses (lah-lee-stuh-day-kooRs) shopping list 9

le lit (luh-lee) bed 1

les livres (m.) (lay-leevR) books 5

la luge (lah-lUj) sled 23

la lumière (lah-lU-myeR) light 21

le lundi (luh-lIIⁿ-dee) Monday 27

la lune (lah-lUn) moon 21

les lunettes (f.) (lay-lU-net) glasses 24

les lunettes de soleil (f.) (lay-lU-net-duh-suh-lay) sunglasses 19

M

la machine à laver (lah-mah-shee-nah-lah-vay) washing machine 12

le maillot de bain (luh-mah-yod-bIⁿ) bathing suit 19

la main (lah-mIⁿ) hand 2, 24

la maison (lah-may-zOⁿ) house 18

le manchot (luh-mAⁿ-sho) penguin 14

manger (mAⁿ-jay) to eat 3

le manteau (luh-mAⁿ-toh) coat 10, 23

les maracas (f.) (lay-mah-Rah-kah) maracas 6

le marchand de fleurs (luh-mahR-shAⁿd-flERR) florist 4, 9

le marchand de fruits (luh-mahR-shAⁿd-fRwee) fruit stand 9

les marches (f.) (lay-mahRsh) steps 21

le mardi (luh-mahR-dee) Tuesday 27

la mare (lah-mahR) pond 7

la marmelade (lah-mahR-muh-lahd) jam 3

le marron (luh-mah-ROⁿ) brown 30

le masque (luh-mahsk) mask 8

le matin (luh-mah-tI^n) morning 25

la mécanicienne (lah-may-kah-nee-syen) mechanic 13

le médecin (luh-mayd-sI^n) doctor 13

le melon (luh-muh-lO^n) melon 11

le menton (luh-mA^n-tO^n) chin 24

le menuisier (luh-muh-nwee-zye) carpenter 13

la mer (lah-meR) sea 19

le mercredi (luh-meR-kRuh-dee) Wednesday 27

la mère (lah-meR) mother 22

le miel (luh-myel) honey 20

le miroir (luh-mee-RwahR) mirror 2, 10

la mobylette (lah-mo-bee-let) scooter 4

les modes (m.) de transport (lay-muhd-duh-trA^ns-puhR) transportation 16

le monde (luh-mO^n-duh) world 13

la montagne (lah-mO^n-tah-nyuh) mountain 18

les moules (f.) (lay-mool) mussels 9

le mouton (luh-moo-tO^n) sheep 20

N

nager (nah-jay) to swim 19

la nappe (lah-nahp) tablecloth 8

naviguer (nah-vee-gay) to sail 16

le navire (luh-nah-veeR) ship 16

la neige (lah-nej) snow 23, 26

neiger (ne-jay) to snow 23

neuf (nuhf) nine 29

le nez (luh-nay) nose 24

le nid (luh-nee) nest 18

le Noël (luh-no-el) Christmas 22

le noir (luh-nwahR) black 30

les notes (f.) (lay-not) notes 6

le nuage (luh-nU-ahj) cloud 23

la nuit (lah-nwee) night 21, 25

les numéros (m.) (lay-nU-may-Ro) numbers 29

O

l'obscurité (f.) (luhb-skU-ree-tay) darkness 21

l'œil (m.) (luhy) eye 24

les œufs (m.) (lay-zuh) eggs 9

l'oiseau (m.) (lwah-zo) bird 17

l'ongle (m.) (lO^ngl) fingernail 24

l'orange (f.) (luh-RA^nj) orange (fruit) 17; orange (color) 30

l'ordinateur (m.) (luhR-dee-nah-tERR) computer 1

l'oreille (f.) (luh-Ray) ear 24

l'oreiller (m.) (luh-Ray-yay) pillow 1

l'ours (m.) (looRs) bear 14

l'ouvrier (m.) (loo-vRee-ye) construction worker 13

P

la paille (lah-pahy) straw 20

le pain (luh-pI^n) bread 17

le panier (luh-pah-nyay) basket 9

le panneau (luh-pah-no) sign 4

le pantalon (luh-pA^n-tah-lO^n) pants 10

les pantoufles (f.) (lay-pA^n-toofl) slippers 1

le paon (luh-pA^n) peacock 20

le papier hygiénique (luh-pah-pyay-eej-yay-neek) toilet paper 2

le papillon (luh-pah-pee-yO^n) butterfly 14

le parasol (luh-pah-Rah-suhl) beach umbrella 19

parler (pahR-lay) to talk 4

la partition (lah-paR-tee-syO^n) score 6

la pastèque (lah-pahs-tek) watermelon 17

la patère (lah-pah-teR) coat hook 5

la patinette (lah-pah-tee-net) scooter 8

les patins (m.) (lay-pah-tI^n) roller skates 7

le peigne (luh-pe-nyuh) comb 2

peigner (pen-yay) to comb 2

peindre (pI^ndR) to paint 13

le peintre (luh-pI^ntR) painter 13

la pelle (lah-pel) shovel 17, 19

la peluche (lah-puh-lUsh) teddy bear 1

la pendule (lah-pA^n-dUl) clock 12

le père (luh-peR) father 22

le père Noël (luh-peR-no-el) Santa Claus 22

le perroquet (luh-pe-Ro-kay) parrot 14

petit (puh-tee) small 10

le petit avion (luhp-tee-tah-vyO^n) light aircraft 16

le petit déjeuner (luhp-tee-day-juh-nay) breakfast 3

le petit garçon (luhp-tee-gahR-sO^n) boy 7

la petite fille (lahp-teet-fee) girl 7

les petits pois (m.) (layp-tee-pwah) peas 17

le phare (luh-fahR) lighthouse 16

le phoque (luh-fuhk) seal 14

le piano (luh-pyah-no) piano 6

le pied (luh-pyay) foot 2

la pierre (lah-pyeR) stone 18

le pigeon (luh-pee-jO^n) pigeon 7

le pirate (luh-pee-Raht) pirate 15

le placard de cuisine (luh-plah-kahR-duh-kwee-zeen) cupboard 12

la plage (lah-plahj) beach 19

la planche à roulettes (lah-plA^n-shah-Roo-let) skateboard 7

la planche à voile (lah-plA^n-shah-vwahl) windsurfing 19

la plante (lah-plA^nt) plant 9

planter (plA^n-tay) to plant 20

le plateau (luh-plah-to) tray 3

la pluie (lah-plwee) rain 26

la poêle (lah-pwahl) frying pan 12

la poire (lah-pwahR) pear 17

le poisson (luh-pwah-sO^n) fish 9, 19

la pomme (lah-puhm) apple 17

la pomme de pin (lah-puhm-duh-pI^n) pinecone 18

la pomme de terre (lah-puhm-duh-teR) potato 11

le pompier (luh-pO^n-pyay) fireman 13

la porte (lah-puhRt) door 3, 20

le portemanteau (luh-puhRt-mA^n-to) hanger 10

le poste de radio (luh-puhst-duh-Rah-dyo) radio 3

la poubelle (lah-poo-bel) garbage can 4, 12

le pouce (luh-poos) thumb 24

la poule (lah-pool) hen 20

le poulet (luh-poo-lay) chicken 9

la poulpe (lah-poolp) octopus 9

la poupée (lah-poo-pay) doll 8

les poussins (m.) (lay-poo-sI^n) chicks 20

prendre (pRA^ndR) to take 11

prendre dans ses bras (pRA^ndR-dA^n-say-bRah) to hug 3

le printemps (luh-pRI^n-tA^n) spring 28

la prise de courant (lah-pReez-duh-koo-RA^n) socket 12

le prix (luh-pRee) price 11

le pull-over (luh-pU-luh-veR) sweater 10, 23

le pyjama (luh-pee-jah-mah) pajamas 1

Q

quatre (kahtR) four 29

la queue (lah-kuh) tail 14

R

le rafraîchissement (luh-Rah-fRay-shees-mA^n) drink 8

le râteau (luh-Rah-toh) rake 19

la règle (lah-Regl) ruler 5

la reine (lah-Ren) queen 15

English-French Glossary

A
afternoon l'après-midi (m.) 25
alarm clock le réveil 1
angel l'ange (m.) 22
ants les fourmis (f.) 18
apple la pomme 17
arm le bras 2, 24
armoire l'armoire (f.) 1
autumn l'automne (m.) 28
axe la hache 17

B
backpack le sac à dos 5, 18
bag le sac 10
bakery la boulangerie 4
ball le ballon 1
balloon le ballon 8
banana la banane 11
basket le panier 9
bat la chauve-souris 21
bathing suit le maillot de bain 19
bathroom la salle de bains 2
bathtub la baignoire 2
beach la plage 19
beach umbrella le parasol 19
bear l'ours (m.) 14
bed le lit 1
bee l'abeille (f.) 18
belt la ceinture 1
bench le banc 7
bicycle la bicyclette 7
big grand 10
bikini le bikini 19
bird l'oiseau (m.) 17
black le noir 30
blackboard le tableau 5
blanket la couverture 1
blind man l'aveugle (m.) 4
to blow souffler 8
blue le bleu 30
boat la barque 16
books les livres (m.) 5
boot la botte 18
bottle la bouteille 11
boy le petit garçon 7
branch la branche 21
bread le pain 17
breakfast le petit déjeuner 3
broom le balai 12
brother le frère 22
brown le marron 30
bucket le seau 7, 19

bus l'autobus (m.) 4, 16
bus stop l'arrêt de bus (m.) 4
butcher's la boucherie 9
butter le beurre 3
butterfly le papillon 14
to buy acheter 9

C
cabin la cabane 21
cake le gateau 8
calendar le calendrier 5
camcorder le caméscope 15
camera l'appareil photo (m.) 8
campfire le feu de camp 21
can la boîte de conserve 11
candle la bougie 8
candy les bonbons (m.) 8, 22
cap la casquette 18
car la voiture 4, 16
card la carte 22
Carnival Time Les fêtes (f.) de Mardi Gras 15
carpenter le menuisier 13
carrot la carotte 11
cart le chariot 9
cash register la caisse enregistreuse 11
cashier la caissière 11
castle le château 1
cat le chat 3, 20
cauliflower la choufleur 17
cell phone le téléphone portable 4
cello le violoncelle 6
cereal les céréales (f.) 3
chair la chaise 5
chair lift le remonte-pente 23
chalk la craie 5
chaperone le chaperon 18
cheek la joue 24
cheese le fromage 9
chicken le poulet 9
chicks les poussins (m.) 20
chimney la cheminée 21
chin le menton 24
chips les chips (m.) 8
chocolate le chocolat 8
chorus le chœur 6
Christmas le Noël 22
Christmas tree le sapin de Noël 22

classroom la salle de classe 5
clock la pendule 12
cloth le chiffon 12
clothes les vêtements (m.) 10
cloud le nuage 23
clown le clown 15
coat le manteau 10, 23
coat hook la patère 5
cold froid 23
colors les couleurs (f.) 30
comb le peigne 2
to comb peigner 2
computer l'ordinateur (m.) 1
conductor le chef d'orchestre 6
construction worker l'ouvrier (m.) 13
to cook cuisiner 12
cook le cuisinier 13
cookies les biscuits (m.) 3
costumes les déguisements (m.) 15
country la campagne 18
cow la vache 20
cowboy le cow-boy 15
crab le crabe 19
credit card la carte de crédit 11
cub le lionceau 14
cup la tasse 3
cupboard le placard de cuisine 12
to cure guérir 13
curtain le rideau 1
cymbals les cymbales (f.) 6

D
to dance danser 15
dancer la danseuse 13
darkness l'obscurité (f.) 21
daughter la fille 22
day le jour 25
decorations les décorations (f.) 22
dentist la dentiste 13
desk le bureau 5
detergent le détersif 11
devil le diable 15
doctor le médecin 13
dog le chien 20
doll la poupée 8
dolphin le dauphin 14
door la porte 3, 20
drawing le dessin 5

to dream rêver 21
dress la robe 10
to drink boire 7
drink le rafraîchissement 8
to drive conduire 16
drum le tambour 6
duck le canard 20

E
ear l'oreille (f.) 24
to eat manger 3
eggs les œufs (m.) 9
eight huit 29
elbow le coude 24
elephant l'éléphant (m.) 14
entrance l'entrée (f.) 11
eraser l'effaceur (m.) 5
eraser la gomme 5
exit la sortie 11
eye l'œil (m.) 24
eyebrow le sourcil 24

F
face le visage 24
fairy la fée 15
farm la ferme 20
farmer le fermier 20
father le père 22
faucet le robinet 17
field le champ 20
finger le doigt 24
fingernail l'ongle (m.) 24
fire le feu 22
fireman le pompier 13
fireplace le foyer 22
firewood le bois à brûler 17, 21
fish le poisson 9, 19
fitting room le salon d'essayage 10
five cinq 29
flashlight la lampe de poche 21
florist le marchand de fleurs 4, 9
flower la fleur 9, 18
flute la flûte traversière 6
to fly voler 16
folder la chemise 5
food les aliments (m.) 12
foot le pied 2
forehead le front 24
forest le bois 18
fork la fourchette 3
fountain la fontaine 7

red le rouge 30
refrigerator le frigo 12
river le fleuve 21
road la chaussée 16
robot le robot 15
rock le rocher 21
roller skates les patins (m.) 7
roof le toit 21
rooster le coq 20
rug le tapis 1
ruler la règle 5
to run courir 7

S
sack le sac 17
sad triste 24
to sail naviguer 16
sailboat le voilier 16
sales clerk la vendeuse 10
sand le sable 19
sand castle le château de sable 19
sandwich le sandwich 7, 8
Santa Claus le père Noël 22
Saturday le samedi 27
sausages les saucisses (f.) 9
scale la balance 11
scarecrow l'épouvantail (m.) 17
scarf l'écharpe (f.) 23
scissors les ciseaux (m.) 5
scooter la mobylette 4; la patinette 8
score la partition 6
sea la mer 19
seal le phoque 14
seasons les saisons (f.) de l'année (f.) 28
see-saw la bascule 7
seven sept 29
sheep le mouton 20
sheet (of paper) la feuille 5
shell la coquille 19
ship le navire 16
shirt la chemise 10
shoe la chaussure 10
shopping les courses (f.) 9
shopping cart le caddie 11
shopping list la liste des courses 9
shoulder l'épaule (f.) 24
shovel la pelle 17, 19
shower la douche 2

sign le panneau 4
to sing chanter 6
singer la chanteuse 15
sink l'évier (m.) 12; le lavabo 2
sister la sœur 22
six six 29
skateboard la planche à roulettes 7
to ski faire du ski 23
skier le skieur 23
skirt la jupe 10
skis les skis (m.) 23
sky le ciel 19
sled la luge 23
to sleep dormir 1
slide le toboggan 7
slippers les pantoufles (f.) 1
small petit 10
snail l'escargot (m.) 18
sneakers les baskets (m.) 1
snow la neige 23, 26
to snow neiger 23
snowball la boule de neige 23
snowman le bonhomme de neige 23
soap le savon 2
socket la prise de courant 12
socks les chaussettes (f.) 1
son le fils 22
speedboat la vedette 16
sponge l'éponge (f.) 2, 12
spoon la cuillère 3
sports les sports (m.) 23
spring le printemps 28
squirrel l'écureil (m.) 18
star l'étoile (f.) 21, 22
steps les marches (f.) 21
stereo la chaîne hi-fi 6
stocking le bas 22
stone la pierre 18
stove la cuisinière 12
straw la paille 20
street la rue 4
streetlamp le réverbère 4
student l'étudiante (f.) 13
to study étudier 5
sugar le sucre 3
summer l'été (m.) 28
sun le soleil 19, 26
Sunday le dimanche 27
sunglasses les lunettes de soleil (f.) 19

swan le cygne 7
sweater le pull-over 10, 23
to sweep balayer 13
to swim nager 19
swing la balançoire 7

T
table la table 12
tablecloth la nappe 8
tail la queue 14
to take prendre 11
to talk parler 4
tambourine le tambourin 6
teacher l'instituteur (m.) 5
teddy bear la peluche 1
ten dix 29
three trois 29
thumb le pouce 24
Thursday le jeudi 27
tiger le tigre 14
tinsel les guirlandes (f.) de Noël 22
toast le toast 3
toilet le W.-C. 2
toilet paper le papier hygiénique 2
tomato la tomate 17
toothbrush la brosse à dents 2
toothpaste le dentifrice 2
towel la serviette de bain 2, 19
toys les jouets (m.) 1
track la voie 16
tractor le tracteur 20
traffic light le feu 4
train le train 16
transportation les modes (m.) de transport 16
tray le plateau 3
tree l'arbre (m.) 21
triangle le triangle 6
truck le camion 4
trumpet la trompette 6
trunk la trompe 14
t-shirt le tee-shirt 10
Tuesday le mardi 27
tunnel le tunnel 16
turtle la tortue 14
two deux 29

U
underpants le caleçon 10

V
vegetables les légumes (m.) 9
vet le vétérinaire 14
violin le violon 6

W
waiter le serveur 13
to wash laver 12
washing machine la machine à laver 12
wastepaper basket la corbeille à papier 5
to water arroser 17
water l'eau (f.) 20
water bottle la gourde 18
water skiing le ski nautique 16
watering can l'arrosoir (m.) 17
watermelon la pastèque 17
wave la vague 19
weather le temps 26
Wednesday le mercredi 27
week la semaine 27
wheelchair le fauteuil roulant 14
white le blanc 30
wind le vent 26
window la fenêtre 20
windsurfing la planche à voile 19
winter l'hiver (m.) 23, 28
winter hat le bonnet de neige 23
witch la sorcière 15
wizard l'enchanteur (m.) 15
world le monde 13
to write écrire 5

X
xylophone le xylophone 6

Y
to yawn bâiller 21
yellow le jaune 30
yogurt le yaourt 3

Z
zoo le jardin zoologique 14